My Sister's Father

Christine Gardiner

Black
Lawrence
Press

www.blacklawrence.com

Executive Editor: Diane Goettel

Cover Design: Nicole Franco
Book Design: Amy Freels

Published 2017 by Black Lawrence Press.
Printed in the United States.

My Sister's Father

For my sisters
Jessica & Lola
and for Catwin,
in memoriam

Contents

Act III

ACT I

When I was locked in the attic, my sister

would slip me the key and my father would find me
empty in the bathtub, tie me into my shoes
and fling me off to a world of school-girl discomfiture
where my sister haunted every reading of the text-
book, and my father was master of ritual
ceremony in the cafeteria, handling the animals
in and out of their cages: birds made of oiled ridges,
the wood-horned jackalope, my sister.

Through the bars, I watched as my sister
reluctantly put her arm to the elbow into a bag.
A black coil of muscle came out with her hand.

Later we learned that snake had swallowed
                                    the basement
where we slept in its innards. Tumorous. Slow.

Five days since I saw my animal.

He sat at the kitchen table and reviewed its contents
like a second child on the day after Christmas.
She opened the cabinet door and slammed it
and opened it so she could slam it again.
Fact moled through the suburbs.
                                        I fell
into a photograph, an armchair; I slept
in that picture of a father's arms. Soft.
What strength was there—gone. We awoke
to hear the door sounding out its function
but could not descibe the room beyond its frame.
The contents remained plain, indifferent objects:
Drain catch. Clothespin. Toaster in a yellow sleeve.
A cut roast. Cold blood on the platter.

When my sister cleared the table of its contents,

our father was so coercive with the broom handle
that even her fingers wept into the dishwater.
She performed each task like a dutiful bear
and afterward she sat to read the paper
but eventually the kitchen chairs began to gray
from the newsprint on her hands. So our father
demanded that she wash her hands before touching
the chairs. That was a rule. Of course there were rules—
how things were and were not to be done—
but she could not get up from her chair
without touching the consequence.

Those mornings, I turned from her
                                    but at night
curled round each other
                    we heard death
                                rattling the attic.

My sister cleaned the chicken like a child

then held the carcass as a grudge, still-born.
She copied out her mother's recipe, but when
fancy clattered in the pantry, she answered.
She asked one thing: a private notary
to test and sanction the affair.
Then made out a list of fears. She feared
the doctors meddled in her business.
She feared she was again with child.
She feared the kettle would cool quick if taken
from the flame. She should have burnt her first
confession but left it innocent among the papers.

Fear bled

in the usual fashion. She never thought.
The day was long, a longing separate from its length.

I look as though I see the ghost

of failure. I write a *yellow house*
upon an *amber hill*. I write a *bean-shaped*
knocker on the *iron door*. I write *tremor*.
Circumstances shudder with the word. Then
Venezuela. I wake up in *Caracas* and am scared.

When I write *you*, there is a hinging. Something trembles

in the hall. A neighbor knocks to offer me
his yellow stare. *You*, of course, do not appear—
though when I genuflect before the granite
statue in the courtyard, Aquarius
drops his heavy vessel in surprise, spilling
stream of consciousness into the penny fountain.
Temperatures perpetual and spring-like.

I wrote.
       The telling of the seeing broke
                    the crisis.

The things we uttered scurried

into the night, where they reproduced
like rumors or were murdered
by the indifference of the world
while our secrets unraveled
elegantly and silent as our father—
spinning invisible webs
on the other side of the wall.

If the threat is a symbol

for violence, and violence
is an emblem of death,
then death is a cipher—
a cat's eye or diamond—
and tomorrow is a hollow
twig in a stand of dead twigs.

Afterwards, my sister said, as though he had died.

Our father fell into bad contract.
What I heard in his voice sounded like a woman.
I maintained correspondence with a stranger.
I held my hands as I almost remembered they had once been held.
Could not find my papers though I looked twice in the same places.
Waited for days that turned to hours.
Looked again.
The light was pendulous, insufferable.
The woman in his voice performed an aria.
I cannot say I was misused.
The letter was illegible but informed my context.
I cupped my hand around the answer so it could not be copied:
I was misused.
Then made a catalogue of bad outcomes.
My sister has a flat foot.
My sister has matted hair.
I do not have a sister.
The doctors suggest exercise.
They say the chemistry is bad between the players.
This disaster as natural as any other.
If my father will be jailed I do not speculate.
I cannot redact what I did not say.
I said, *I hope.*
I said, *Of course.*
I wandered through an empty vestibule that echoed full of violence.
My sister, I said uneasily, *can this be love?*
Surely, my sister said, *this must be love.*

Money comes into the room and extends

a long hand of invitation. Our father
antes up my trust, and the cards snap back
from the table. Our father palms his two-faced
coin. I can still forgive my first misgivings,
but then every second slanders memory.
Our father bets two hands dealt the absent players,
and Money calls his bluff. I know the flush corrupts,
but if our father does not win, I will be punished

so I shut up like a clam opens into the two halves

of having it or going without. Then Money makes
a note of obligation, and the coin toss drops
between two straight lines marked *ought* and *ought not.*
When I ask *how will it end?* it has ended already.

All night we heard screams

from the yard, and at dawn
we found my animal—
skinned and skewered on a picket.

Daddy has his funny ways.

Daddy walks above the city on a path made of glass.
Daddy builds a cage to cage the day.
When Daddy speaks, a bird with two beaks.
Daddy is a manager of grand affairs.
Daddy makes a boat with tiny paper sails.
Daddy's model never fails, but when it fails
Daddy charters Charon's ferry
down the Schuylkill to the Delaware.
Daddy straddles centuries and stumbles.
Daddy, running backwards up the downward moving stairs.
Daddy holds the handgun. Daddy holds his tongue.
Daddy has a purpose. Daddy has two girls.
Daddy, I don't like this
world.

I watched my sister watch my father waiting

for the elevator in an airport
on the television in the living room.
There was chain-link by the sandlot
and a starship and a robot, but
I could only see the flicker of my father
in the hallway, with his black assault dogs
heaving thickly through their tusks and
his broken lion chained up in the coat closet.
Still my feet were set in concrete,
and I turned so slowly from one problem
to the other that I was frozen solid
at their center, and the whole world
came into an indolent orbit around me.

And I knew the walls were closing in

because the harlequin darkling beetles
flashed the portent, and because they lashed
electric with their iridescent wings,

and because the walls were closing in.

We were cloistered at these interstices
like demons with neatly pleated wings.
My sister was assisted to the ceiling
as I floated backward on my back
above the driveway like a vehicle
of transient romance or nuclear family—
perfectly balanced and ready to detonate
like the matchbox car bomb I watched my father
stitch into my sister's intestines or

the cursed words he inscribed in the veins

of the trees in the backyard, where
the sycamore disguised a secret passage
to the hallway, where I watched my sister
watch my father through the keyhole.

He stood on his toes and deliberately
folded the handgun into the bedding
on the top shelf of the linen closet
in the bathroom. Then let himself
out the window. We went back to bed,
but in the morning, our father was there,
the gun was gone, and the linen closet
had evaporated from the bathroom.

It was hard to know what we knew we saw.

ACT II

Everywhere was elsewhere. Somewhere

hid between the night and mourning.
Everywhere were things to do
worth doing. I did them.
Sat straight. Cut a quarter moon from tinfoil.
Hastened through the tenses.

Everywhere was a system

of boxes. The television stationed
in the living room. The living room installed
within the high-rise. The towers stacked
like city blocks. The entire plot embedded in
the television. The coffer of the mind.

Elsewhere was a square
grave gated by hydrangea.

The backyard was a suburban diner wedged

between Tuesday night and Wednesday morning.
The sky was strung between the signposts. The pine trees
smelled like vinyl. The hallway was a hot expanse
of highway that led only to another nowhere, where
I paced a moral spectrum, but that straight and narrow
alleyway soon turned into discovery:
the business of our sector was well lit but empty
and brutal forces were manipulating its periphery.
My sister lit a cigarette. She turned to me
and whispered through her breath, "What is the color of regret?"
Already she was drowning off the shore of judgment's distant island
and I was driving straight to a policed state of despair, where
hot pink and forever, the vulva wept red
leather seats in the back of a parked convertible sports car.
Time went in and out of focus.
We were ten. She was eleven. I was twelve.
Bleeding through my underclothes.
The mind swam in boyfriends, and flesh swung from the bones of the old.
The dawn was cold and the lawn was frosted over with forgetting.
I caught my sister talking to the mirror eerily.

We love each other don't we?

Then shut up and kiss me like TV.

Behind this gilded stage of imitation, waits

a dressing scene of bird-legged girls. Below
the iron trunks of high tar throwers, one
sister winds her tinny acrobatics through
the spindles, while the other poles
the copper underbelly of a log.

At the metrical foot of the mountain,
the moon describes circumference to the yellow-
whites of the eye, while the mute brown
goose recites a sad amendment to the script
that she is practicing for autumn. When

it all collapses into metaphor,
you and I remain—two halves of the red apple
low hung in the ripening season.

Clocks esconced on all the walls.

Time deviates in passing room to room.
Half past half past two. Now interim takes over.
Two-fifty-two. When bridges break like promises.
A quarter til the count comes back
                              inexorably wrong.
We seize the crisis a hundred times in hindsight,
but when we sit at the same table
our thoughts are not in the same place.
So it goes that
                    what goes unsaid degrades
the palate of the orator—a plate
ruptured along the fault lines
of speech planned but failed
in its delivery to the auditor. Our prescience
does not make a science. We forget.

My father hazards days in revolution.

He circumvents the pathways
of convention. A man about shaking
hands. Swollen with poverty. Cupping
the bottle. A cat in the garden. My father.
He converses eerily with birds.

As if there were no
                        balance to the powers,
he is present even in his absence.
He makes the seasons statically resolve.
He cultivates his absence in the presence of

a walled city beset by falling walls.

My father sees who needs defending.
                                A girl
caught on the ledge that carves the gardens
of remembered from forgetting.

I study the art of moods. Technically it is

my sister's science. Together we experiment
with cunning.
                We devise unfathomable
aims composed of questions.

My sister is familiar with the theories.
Sculptress of the spiritualist medium.
Sentient. Chemically self-possessed.
I sequester every periodic element, while
she inverts the process of discovery.
In theory
                my sister knows how every mystery
is accomplished. How violence can be financed
by the threat of violence. How definite the present
disappearance of our aims. While I

observe the bloated questions
floating to the surface of our answers.

Not in the dim, pointed face of the woman.

Not one cloud upon the dawning of his perfect vision.
Not thriving in the fishery. Not foreplay in the hot-house.
Not mechanical crescendo or unnatural advantage.
Not dialogue. Not duty. Not sickness from the wandering.
Not taxonomy of convalescence. Not amenome.
Not crocus. Not forget-me-not. Never fennel.
Not empty-handed at the breakfast table. No. Not I.
Not yet fallen to the fathom's depth.
Not the fiction of a future nor our mutually funded sorrow.
Not rutted landscapes foreclosing on our decade.
Not the high, upward slope that never peaked.
Neither vultures circling our zenith
nor tragic players dressed in starry gestures.

I apprehend the anxiety of knowing only

apprehension: the quiet where panic
takes root. Propriety insists in one dimension
while sentiment inclines in two and three
concurrent planes. Progress culls a pattern
from the discord; the pattern benefits
from altitude. I fall, but love is not
a precipice—meaning meaning
cannot ascend the given metaphor
and saying says a labyrinth that recoils
from the center of veracity, while
my father paces like a dignitary
on the terrace of uncertainty and mutters:
Tomorrow is a contract that expired.

Four years ago I made that forgery.

I did it. Doubt persisted. For awhile
it seemed the only variable
in our constant circumstance:
the same dolorous inquiry, the same
passive wrestling, the voice of the father
dictating necessity, and I, answering.
                                 I answered.
I raised and I lowered and lowered again
before raising the pen. I made the mark and
                                  resigned
I let drop the banal, hay-colored hand.

Still the archeologist lived downstairs
and the recluse split logs in the yard.
Birds fixed and unfixed patterns on the wire.
Bills arrived by mail. In silence, I listened
and listened without knowing what for.

The telephone called, and reception

soon replaced the shuffling of papers on the desk.
My sister welcomed popular opinion but knew better
than to reply directly to such notions.
Instead she copied out the variegated details
and put those methods into practice,
but when she tried to balance her accounts,
every word exchanged made the possibility of trade invalid.
All my sister had was language, and her language had no currency,
so she stacked the coded letters into coded, well-stacked piles,
then received an inbox full of backslashes. Dust gathered.
My sister did not know what else to do and so did nothing.
Outside, the workers washed the windows.
                                        Beyond the glass,
another world spread another plate of glass.

O Sound Logic! O Well-Divisioned Labor!

O Hand-Held Cellular Device! O Digital Imagery!
O Collagen! O Exposé! O Real Time!
O Embezzled Victory! Conditioned Anonymity!
O Semblance between Executive and Execute!
O Sluggardly Consumption and Dastardly Collateral!
O Off-Balance Balance Sheet! O Righteous Public Outrage!
O Abandoned Homeland Cul-de-Sac! Our Collapsing Physic State!
O Silenced Opposition! O Failure Despite Trying!
O Generation of Emergency Generators! O Militant Factions!
O Hardened Feelings! Disconsolate Enemy! O False Belief!
O Daughter of Sorrows! You, who would engender future
daughters! O Pardon your Bequest! O Other Cheek!

Hazard settles on the Cornice of Discovery.

Hazard lights the Highway in Formation.
Hazard terminates the painted Landscape.
Hazard squats. Hazard straddles Opposition.
Hazard fights the Safety of the Setting.
Hazard states its Case in Tongues.
Hazard wastes. And Hazard threatens Peril.
Hazard signs the Cross. Hazard writes the Wrong.
Hazard hazards Mercy and repents.
Hazard makes the Resolution miscarry.
Hazard pictures Books in incensed Piles.
Hazard inserts the Dreamer in the Dream.
Then Hazard turns the Axle in the Linchpin.
The Linchpin turns and in the turning destines.

As my father hedged around the meaning

of the hedges, funds dropped out of the market
as if the market were a university or window
from which my father watched red hawks
soar like price above the Hudson.

Flights chartered by the changing trade winds.

My father tallied up his pickets and his thimbles,
but when the nest egg dropped onto the sidewalk
all solvency ran off into the gutter as if

it were my father's fault that he defaulted
on the loan, when this fault I credit
to the daughter who has fallen underwater
where debenture swims a cold horizon cut by headlines:

THE GLACIAL CREDIT MARKET THAWS.

The floe
        dislodged the day
                from recompense.

Something happened in the room when I left the room.

I passed certain landmarks. I did it with pause.
I smelled it. The weather was variable.
The trouble is the problem was compounded.
My sister turned the words over with tongs.
One term conflated with all others.
Overheard the unvoiced judgment of the judges.
Looked back but could gauge no progress in the discord.
I signed my father's hand.
Everything was resolved. The resolution was not everything.
The finale was inferred from the first word.
The document insinuates the present.
Not memory that abates but its efficacy.
My father, divested of his outfit.

The past. Half a tapestry hung on a dusty loom.

A gallery of spinning light.
A span of a span of days.
One spinster who snips the vanishing threads.
Two sisters who iron the air.
Three wishes locked in a box.
A box of ciphers.
A box of pins and needles.
A box of loss.
Intimate noises like an opening seam.
A gold lynx crouched in the corner.
Outside, the tinny sound of a parade.
Our emperor, arrayed in airy finery.
That fated charade.

His time had finally come

into the living room and settled
like an elephant in the corner.
Evidence there hidden
in plain vision.
We read the paper
trail for a beginning, but
that ancient scroll unrolled
in all dimensions, so we ran
from the summons.
We ran from our name.
We married; it stuck.
We shouldn't have converted.
Wherever we ran, our hearts were penned
like sows in the sentence:

OUR FATHER STANDS ON TRIAL FOR HIS ERRORS

and the internet never forgets it.

We stood at the edge of that precipice.

Our father held his hollow ground.
My sister stood diminutive for sorrow.
                              She sighed
and looked up at me through my eyes.
I stood stock-still, frozen like an animal
that would go invisible if I refused to move.

In this way, we all adopted common postures of denial.

I became a lie detector. My sister

was my father's answering machine.
He processed all my sister's words
before she said them. She was the personal
computer of his interests. He controlled it all
remotely, while she, obsequious, disposed
the heavy garbage
                                    but never could escape
the fires he had started in the basement.

I tried to be the type of writer
that could write our type of failure
but all my trying failed because our story
was alive with buried secrets worming towards
the daylight, and I was just reading the papers.

So take my hands and pull my strings.
Pull my pretty hair in handfuls.
Pull to see how much will come.
Withdrawing funds.

Calculate expended grief and total sin.

You are a shop-keep sweeping up
the order of the cosmos closing in.

Then frown and listen harder to the rain.

The rose hedge by the window ledge
is hung with dew, and through this lens
which magnifies our pain, you scan
the stories of the house that housed our clan

where public scandal rained in righteous anger,

winds unhinged the secrets in the cabinet,
ignominy felled the family tree, and
the roof collapsed beneath his reputation.

Rumor spread like water over floorboards.
My sister blotted at the mess with bulletins:

A FATHER RAINING DIAMONDS ON HIS DAUGHTERS!
A FATHER PICKING POCKETS! OUR FATHER IS A FRAUD!

We thought, perhaps, the storm would pass
and history would arch over us
in all the colors of the covenant

but the moral of our story was
our story had no moral, so
the rains soaked through
our marble mansion made
of cardboard. We poured
our soiled wishes in the fishbowl
and climbed another cobbled
ladder propped to nowhere

where the future was a stranger
ready in the pantry
with a yardstick, waiting to assess
the difference between what happened
and what was said to have happened
last fiscal year.
               The year of the rat,
                              now past.

ACT III

There was no map. It was all go and go—

—and see how far—and where—the going got,
until every endeavor was lost in a maze
of covered terraces, closets, gondolas, and granite statues,
and then—to the amazement of the starlings—
the sky tumbled into a puddle in the gutter,
and the world was reduced to its miniature:

tiny burnished reliquaries,
                    nearly invisible pyramids,
                                        etc.,

but in every memory, my sister remains a human tower
that fell only for mysterious ideals, reasons
I understood by intuition could not explain with words,
because her hunger was a hunger beyond language,
and her most transparent gesture was the translation
of the scarab's carapace into the porcelain basin.

To set out. To aviate the classic passions.

To plumb the depths of reticence. To isolate the thrusting
left hip from the right. To quantify time difference
with a yardstick. To map the rugged landscape of
the sentence. To smooth the middle distance like a flat sheet.
To approach the problem in full uniform. To menace.
To shoot the lunar saucer off the mesa. To turn conviction over
like a bowl. To wrap the winter solstice in aluminum.
To ration scandal. To string the sky along the clothesline.
To knot the strands of artificial light. To make money
like a promise. To lean against the gravestone as
you lean back in the chair. To put the final word down
like a shell. To read the signals wrought by drifting
vapors. To mislay infinity in those whorls.

When the garbled tracks branch

organic blooms marked *you* and *I*,
we stem: baroque, nostaglic roses—then fail
like constructions made of paper.
Split hairs. Fruit halved by the blade.
I read the schedule for a way out

but only indecision meets me at the station so

I follow your thought into another country
where time comes and goes without a ticket.

The past is a map of missed connections,
good intentions capsized in the swimming pool.
You knot whatever frontier lines my circumspection.
Mouths open and are closed as automatic doors.
Not the sentence that fragments. Its desire.

The ramp made a downward spiral meant

to represent the saga of the cosmos.
I swallowed, and the planetarium stuck
in my throat. What I did not say I saved
for later. What was left went bad before
the thaw in January froze.

Another hour passed by like a pick-up.

Mars was a glass cave I mined for gold,
then splintered. Later, I would confuse that moment
with a pornographic movie, though when
I called to cancel the affair, then the moving
corridor was moving with me,
and love was just another thing that happened—
an accident—the act of growing old.

One yellow bloom becomes a referent for the other.

Old memory assumes the new dimensions of an attic room.
Here is another bowl of dust. Here another spoon.
One lover hastens down the corridor and disappears.

When the other turns the knob, I balk. This is another way
of dancing, though we stay essentially the same.
We whisper at each other in the night. We are scared.

We are made of legs. The legs are braided through the covers.
I slide my feet into the other woman's shoes but feel the same
old disappointment in the union. The same sore indecision.
And other points on which we disagree. The yellow pages

fade like yellow roses, withered by the death-bed
where my old man pled for one more kiss.
Then another and another. And please. Another kiss.

The high road delved, divulging.

Then it flattened. We stalled. The mist
came up in currents off the mountain.
One swan hovered in the gully, and the dawn
spilled luminous oil on the floor.

We passed through the dirty filling station door.

The bell sounded the same to signal
our advancements, your withdrawal.

I took your hand and turned it over on the landing

but my fortune-telling told our story wrong
and the hieroglyph appearance of the palm
revealed only the grievance of foreknowing:

You would not be in my audience.
Attentive. Leaning forward toward tomorrow.

Your hands were cold unwieldy instruments

I had forgotten how to play, and though we could not
see through the window to its origin, light
urinated on the escalator, bore us
to different levels of a problem
we soured of hearing. Then the note broke
through, the belt snapped, and you appeared
pounding on the glass aquarium until
a fissure resulted in the mirror of your eye
reflecting the ugly fabric, our daily custom
wore it to rags, flapped like a bird
around the clear confines of the mind,
cawing echoes of what we were
when we were one figure—in that era.

My sister read the rearview for an answer

to the future, but the highway was a filmstrip
of a strip mall. Skipping like Nebraska on repeat.

My sister counted down the exits on her fingers.
She tallied up our problems two by two.
I blinked. She looked like a hired typist

in the front seat. Or a tired, non-committal hypnotist.
Quickly slipping her desires through the loopholes.
Revising the horizon on the billboards.

I blinked, and through fluorescent mist, I saw
the girl I had been watching the whole time
who was my sister and was gone—

off to the empty storefront in the backseat, where
forever knocks the wrong side of locked doors.

My sister left home to learn about fear

but only when she returned did she find it, rocking
in a chair by the window. It was then she caught
her finger in the secret of his hinged credenza

and experienced the coffin

as simultaneous with marigolds and profit.
Abruptly she saw through our opulent interior
to its foundation in sorcery and jailors,
warfare and bare-faced mountains. She watched
the equator wrap its firm girdle around the waste
of the earth. The night was a shadow, a spell
cast by the earth, and the moon—a loose,
wandering wheel on a horse-drawn hearse,
creaking over the low, silver cover of snow.

My father left a letter for my sister

on the counter, among other artifacts
and shadows. A spindle. A thimble.
The bowl of her hands. The heart is a pot
of violets withered in the corner where
she read it. His pale, inarticulate light.
Shivering. Bereft of depth.

A sentiment
              tardily expressed
                          of regret.

It may seem that I know what stories to tell
but the truth is like a seam of light
that retreats from approach down the tiled
floor in the hall, a sense of foreboding

or molar, yellow and eaten with holes,
lost under the deathbed, found as a pearl.

Finished the story but lost in the midst of it.

A lonely child, wandering the cosmos.
Past the eyes of the aspen.
Sibilant pines.
The gold horizon.
Our only parameter.
A wall—passive—upholding its purpose.
A cold house full of things.
Fear pacing the room like an animal.
Illegible gestures.
Shadows in the attic.
A gunshot.
The scream of a train.
Writing the inevitable in order to prevent it.
The next page blank with darkness.

Clouded eyes the color

of a cloud. Hands so cold,
   if he touched her eyes,
   her eyes would snow.

To hear the sea, press

your ear to the shell
of a spiritual man.

Laughter echoes its proximity to slaughter.

How the horror started with a dollar.
How it ended sometime after breakfast on a Wednesday.
A sound in the corridor, drowned out by the sound of the train.
Then silence, coiled in the talons of the rafters.
Fish-eyed suicide.
Hooked on the line of consequence.
Radiant spring.
Numb summer.
The days wearing airily away.
I am full.
An empty feeling of dread emptied of language.
How we shared a certain quality of being.
The closed, private odor of sleep.

You return, in your mind, to a room filled with people

you used to know. It is a cold, dusty chamber arranged
with common strangers, and poised in the spotlight is the withered
woman of your adolescence, so you ask her the series of inevitable,
unconscionable questions, and she confesses a secret
you cannot understand, and suddenly she is you, and you are me,
and we are weeping in the middle of the sex act,
raw on the sea wall behind another theatre of illusions,
saying no to the act but not meaning it,
committing the act and waiting for the act to be over.
Then you are running away without knowing what towards.
The hour is midnight, the dark is a maze of spring flowers,
and you are lost in a complex of dream-rooms,
locked with the bear in her caravan, chained to the door
of a dressing room in a department store where you are preparing
for your performance at the lawyer's summer cottage.
You fear that you will fail to please the crowd, so you fail
to please the crowd, then wind the desperate circlet of the racetrack
around your ankle and shrug your shoulders off the skyway,
where you are hitchhiking or you are picking up hitchhikers,
and when you are finally confronted by the bald certainty
of his faded pate, you don't know what your father is trying to say
because you cannot hear his muted voice through the glass
wall between you, so you telephone and leave a message at the tone.
Then put your guard down like a glove, just for a moment,
but everyone is talking over you, pretending not to understand
the only question worth asking, which you have already forgotten,
and, anyway, the sky above you is indecent and a rag,
and you are prostrate below it, impossibly positioned
in every possible position, watching as I drop words like stones
into the hole that you hollowed out for the purpose of filling
with something peculiar, redundant, inimitable, dull.

When the forsythia has finished with its yellow spectacle,

when the sofa whispers peonies and roses,
when the bed sheets are laced with dainty cobwebs,
when these layers of formal scenery, one after another, fall away,
when the lavender nursery collapses on the marble stairwell,
and comprehension cracks the bathroom mirror of her eyes,
when you have cultivated a deadly suspicion of housecats and tragedy
and seven years bad luck can only diminish your sense of foreboding,
when you have gone room by room through your volume of memories,
when you have searched every revelation for clues but found none,
when the catafalque has been wheeled with finality into the foyer,
and the cloisonné ossuary is flanked by dead orchids,
only then will your sister emerge from closed quarters
to pace the quivering lip of the world—invisible, mute.

The past consumes the past

is tense; the future slinks
on tiptoe to the present,
which disintegrates
like paper insect wings
between uncertain fingers,

but time is the infinitive:

to thread forever
through a sentiment like
milk quartz, embedded
in the sediment.

Whether yours is a set of rules set down to be broken

or a fixed game of extortion,
whether your inheritance derives from the fated passage of generations
or one thing leading simply to another,
whether you are dressed in leather or lace
or a paper dress spread demurely over the edge of the sickbed,
whether you receive a postmarked notice of foreclosure
or a charred, well-whittled effigy,
whether you frame photographs of futures past
or concoct other unpleasant ways to please her,
whether these words are the echo of his sticky hardwood dictates
or a scrawl from her horror show diary,
whether you suffer the backhanded luck of the draw
or rearrange the scattered pieces of our puzzlement,
whether the weather is grim or resplendent,
whether you examine a casket, an urn, or a handful of dust,
whether the scent wafts from a deodorized ailment
or an array of cut flowers,
whether you are a young girl in trouble
or a wild hen thatching her nest,
whether you uncover the process of becoming
or listen to the dull hum of nothing,
whether memory is comprehensive or empty,
whether you repent or are shamed,
whatever you do, letters arrive addressed to the dead.

My sister retreats to the vanishing point.

My father sleeps, diminished, in the foreground.
I navigate the vacancy between them like

an iridescent beetle, trapped
between the window and the screen.
Scanning the horizon for its origin.

Progress idles in fluorescent
revolutions like the ceiling fan.
Locked in a cage of days.

Stale drone of August.
Clouds orbit. Light blurs.
I flick the desiccated ornament away.

He hovers above a puddle of blood.
She hollows the bones of the birds.

You trifle and chance, until

one day you are underwater, where
the silence is noisome and din,
and the light—strewn like split cords
on the workshop floor—dims
and dims further, until the body
is just another form of abandon,
and you sense the swollen heart
first plummet, then rise
to the still, scarred surface of being,
where impermeable and quivering,
inexplicable as the seraph,
it quacks and buoys like a duck.

This is the way the ladies ride.

Early Sunday morning, I rode among the gentlemen.
I leaned in and spoke close to the eyes. I watched
the little cowgirls ride upstairs. Thick, red wrists
and shingled nails. My father was a weightless
sailboat, anchored to his customary chair.
The phone rang, and the kettle decanted
a cup full of air.
                 My sister turned and whispered:
It's for you, but I heard only the silent drone
of no one moaning: *You are your father's daughter.*
You are. You are your father's daughters.

Gracefully he demonstrated how to float away
but when the spirit lingered at the threshold to the garden,
I stepped over.
             A gold curtain of light closed,
                        enclosed me.

Acknowledgements

Some of these poems were previously published in *Rio Grande Review*, *Catch Up*, and in the 2009 chapbook "Poems from My Sister's Father," published by the inimitable Sarah Stone. Thank you to these editors for publishing this work.

"The high road delved, divulging" alludes to "The Filling Station" by Elizabeth Bishop; "To set out. To aviate the classic passions" draws inspiration from *The Art of War* by Sun Tzu; and "As my Father hedged around the meaning of the hedges" was written in response to *The New York Times* coverage of the financial crisis of 2008. "This is the way the ladies ride" refers to the nursery rhyme of the same name.

Thank You

I would not have been able to write this book without the generous support of Brown University's Department of the Literary Arts and the Division of Arts, Humanities, & Social Sciences at the University of Denver. Thank you to my teachers for their guidance and for giving me the permission I needed to channel this work, especially Joanna Howard, Brian Evenson, Kevin McLaughlin, Bin Ramke, Selah Saterstrom, Eleni Sikelianos, Diana Sullivan, Keith & Rosmarie Waldrop, and CD Wright. I am grateful to my colleagues from Brown, DU, and CNR, whose vision and poetics helped shape this manuscript and to my friends for their abundant love and support. Special thanks to my talented and generous collaborators Emily Dryden, Nicole Franco, and Will Godfrey. Love to Christian. Thanks to Joanna Ruocco, Patty Godfrey Ko, and Erica Ko. Love and gratitude to Marream Krollos.

This book deals in complex themes, and I want to thank my family—especially Mom and James—for their patience and understanding as I wrote to unearth my truth.

Photo: Emily Dryden

Christine Gardiner holds a BA and MFA from Brown University and a PhD from the University of Denver. She lives in Brooklyn and is an Assistant Professor of the Liberal Arts at the College of New Rochelle, School of New Resources, where she is edified by her students and their stories.